Angela MacLauchlan

One Step At A Time

Living With Ataxia
and Multiple System
Atrophy

WESTBOW
P R E S S®
A DIVISION OF THOMAS NELSON
& ZONDERVAN

Scripture taken from the New King James Version. Copyright 1979, 1980,
1982 by Thomas Nelson, inc. Used by permission. All rights reserved.

This book is a work of non-fiction. Unless otherwise noted, the author
and the publisher make no explicit guarantees as to the accuracy of
the information contained in this book and in some cases, names
of people and places have been altered to protect their privacy.

NAF's "Understanding Genetics"

WestBow Press books may be ordered through booksellers or by contacting:

WestBow Press
A Division of Thomas Nelson & Zondervan
1663 Liberty Drive
Bloomington, IN 47403
www.westbowpress.com
1 (866) 928-1240

Because of the dynamic nature of the Internet, any web addresses or
links contained in this book may have changed since publication and
may no longer be valid. The views expressed in this work are solely those
of the author and do not necessarily reflect the views of the publisher,
and the publisher hereby disclaims any responsibility for them.

ISBN: 978-1-5127-4333-3 (sc)
ISBN: 978-1-5127-4332-6 (e)

Library of Congress Control Number: 2016908213

Print information available on the last page.

WestBow Press rev. date: 06/20/2016

Contents

Foreword

Angela MacLauchlan's book "One Step at a Time" details the path which led to the discovery of an obscure brain disorder that would change her life.

Multiple system atrophy and ataxia are so rare that even the neurologists Angela consulted were dubious at first about what was causing her mysterious symptoms.

There followed several anxious years for Angela and her family, with numerous visits to medical professionals, trying to find the elusive answer.

Despite many episodes of frustration and no helpful advice, she persisted in trying to find an explanation, and was tested and eventually diagnosed with sporadic Olivopontocerebellar atrophy (OPCA). This was the beginning of a new phase for Angela: living with multiple system atrophy (MSA), and dealing with the many changes it would make to her daily life.

This thoughtful and optimistic book describes her coping strategies, and shows her continuing love of life despite having a rare and debilitating illness. Her faith in God, her unfailing courage, and her joy and optimism, give real meaning to the word "inspirational".

Having been diagnosed with the rare brain disorder spinocerebellar ataxia, I found a lot of personal inspiration from this book, and it is a very enjoyable read despite the serious subject matter.

I am sure that anyone learning to manage and adjust to life with a chronic illness will really appreciate Angela's sensible approach to daily activities, her sense of humor, and above all her steady faith in God. This book will help them find more strength and perseverance to overcome their own struggles.

Terri Heffernan 2015

A Note from My Son David

I have never really understood ataxia and MSA until my mother was diagnosed with the condition. It was extremely difficult and still is, dealing with the conditions and life changing experiences my mum is going through. I can only imagine how hard it must be going from normal day-to-day tasks to not being able to carry them out.

My mum's inner belief and faith have kept her strong during this difficult time and I can't thank mum enough for everything she has done and still does for me, while dealing with her own personal problems.

My step-dad David has been mum's rock, I have the utmost respect for him helping my mum when I couldn't be there for her. Skype has helped mum cope with the distance between us and keep in regular contact.

Not a day goes by that I don't think about my mum and the good old days, carrying the shopping back home and being chased up the stairs in Birch Road. My mum's strength is incredible and I can't believe how strong she is, as I don't think I could deal with the cards my mum has been dealt.

My mother is an inspiration, and if I were a woman I'd like to be like my mum.

David Carson

A Note from My Friend Cassie

"One Step at a Time, Living with Ataxia and Multiple System Atrophy", by Angela MacLauchlan, serves as a helpful and inspiring guide for anyone desiring to learn about ataxia and multiple system atrophy. Angela's book is inspiring in her ability to explain ataxia and MSA while showing her readers her true spirit of joy, peace and love.

"One Step at a Time, Living with Ataxia and Multiple System Atrophy" is informative and a helpful guide to better understanding ataxia and MSA.

Cassie Joyce Hedrick

Acknowledgements

All proceeds from this book will be going to the NAF (National Ataxia Foundation) and the MSA (Multiple System Atrophy) Coalition.

I thought, "Why not just donate the money that it will cost to publish this book," but I would still want to explain to the kids what effects ataxia has on their mum. As they all live in different towns this is the best way, and it will also benefit future generations.

This way too — I hope this book is beneficial to people who have ataxia themselves, care-givers, family members, friends — to give them an idea of what this condition can do to someone. Everyone can be affected in various ways and degrees. This is how ataxia has affected me.

It would be easy to get depressed or feel down over what you hear about ataxia, because a textbook or the internet says this and that will happen, but it does not mean it <u>will</u>. As I said, ataxia differs from person to person. How many doctors are affected by ataxia; are they going by personal experience or by textbook? The best ones to know about ataxia are the people who have got it.

For people who have ataxia, or someone they know has ataxia, or they care for someone who has ataxia, there are online support groups you or they can join.

One of the online support groups is mostly a great bunch of people; you can ask any question and there is always someone who can help answer your question. As I have said before, the best person to answer any question is someone who actually has ataxia.

Thank you so much for being allowed to use the NAF and the MSA logos.

Many thanks to Dr Susan Perlman for all her help in answering my questions about ataxia. She really helped to clear the muddy waters, for it to make sense regarding this matter, not just to me but people who had never even heard of ataxia. How much I didn't know about ataxia, and I had lived with it a few years prior.

I would like to take this opportunity to thank my friend Terri for all the editing she had to do for me, and it was a lot. I'm no writer, and it showed. Terri made it look more professional.

I would also like to take this opportunity to thank my husband David. He is one of the most patient and understanding men I know; nothing seems to faze him and he has had me to put up with.

Lastly, I'm thankful for the internet; it cuts out a lot of the groundwork. The downside to the internet was the amount of reading one can do — there was a lot, and then to try and put it all in to words that were easily understood.

Thank you all.

Angela MacLauchlan, 2015

Introduction

This book was written for my sons — James, Andrew, David, Paul and Ricky.

I couldn't explain much about ataxia; what it is, how ataxia affects someone with it, so what better way than to write a book about it. It is easier to read about it than have me babble on trying to explain ataxia, making it as clear as mud.

This book began with me writing it just for my kids, printing it out and give that to them, then a book form would be better for the grand-kids or future generations to read. Easier to stick a book on a shelf or in a drawer than trying to keep a piece of paper intact. Also, by this time the book had "grown arms and legs", so to speak. My friends and family might be interested in reading it also, as well as other people being interested, and in this way it could help to increase awareness of ataxia. Even if nobody wanted to actually read the book, just by buying it — the proceeds can help towards research into ataxia and multiple system atrophy.

I originally began writing this book 3 or 4 years ago. I stopped writing it about 15 months ago, but I was always going to start it up again as the Spanish say: "mañana" (tomorrow). I had heard on the radio a few times over the last couple of months about God's gifts, and then I heard about how you should use them for other people. When I prayed, I asked God what He wanted me to do – and the word "book" kept coming to mind. I would think to myself, "Oh that ... yeah ... someday I will get around to it."

Over the last few weeks the word "book" kept coming back into my mind, or I met people who had written books; it always just seemed to be about books in some form. Talk about getting prodded with a stick — that's what it felt like. So I have started on it again and now I do have peace about it; it doesn't keep popping into my mind like it used to.

God is always right, even when we think we know better.

I am now 53 years old. I have a twin brother and four other brothers. I have given birth to 5 children — James 35, Andrew 34, David 31, Paul 29 and Ricky 28. So far I have six grandchildren — 14, 13, 13, 9, 7 and 6 years old. Mind you, by the time I have actually finished this book the kids will be nearing 100 years old, and I might even be a great-gran. I am thankful I was able to have the kids and then be blessed with grandkids.

None of them has any health issues regarding ataxia that I know of, I am thankful for that too. Ataxia seems to start and end with me.

I was born in Glasgow and brought up in Montrose which is on the northeast of Scotland.

I have lived in various parts of the United Kingdom, but settled in Cumbernauld about 13 miles from Glasgow. I worked as a bookkeeper full-time for 8 years in a family owned business. Anything that was to be done in an office, you did it, as you were the only one in it. I loved that job, even watched the pet pooch when my boss and his family went on their holidays. That pet pooch "Rico" was a real cutie. The boss was the best I have ever had. I also worked as a security guard a few weekends in summer, doing concert gigs that were mostly in England. Glastonbury and Reading were the two biggest ones.

This book is about how ataxia has affected me and still does. It is not a text book or medical book on ataxia. I don't know the ins and outs of how the brain works — that I leave up to the experts.

There's a chapter describing what ataxia is. I have tried to write about ataxia in a simpler form than what usually has been written about it, so it is easier to try and understand what ataxia is and how it does affect people with it, because ataxia does affect people and the people around them. It's surprising how many people have never heard of ataxia, let alone know what it is.

One of the things I learnt was that OPCA is not exactly what I thought it was. Dr Susan Perlman[1] could not have explained it more clearly than she did, so that I actually understood it. Dr Perlman really knows her stuff; being a specialist in the field of ataxia, Dr Perlman really did help me make sense of it.

There is a chapter about my mobility aids, oh and how I have come too really like them. At first it was 'I don't need them' or 'I don't want them', but a few falls and broken bones sure changed my attitude about that. You really have to think of your safety.

One thing about having ataxia for me is— when things begin to stop working, they stop working whether you want them to or not. Oh, you can go for a while, exercise, diet and resting etc., and doing those things can prolong things, in my case anyway I think it has. I used to walk everywhere, from childhood to a few years ago when I couldn't walk any more. I really loved walking, and could walk miles too, and sometimes I would run. Now I can't really stand unaided for more than a few seconds.

---

[1] Dr Susan L. Perlman, M.D. Clinical Professor of Neurology. David Geffen School of Medicine at UCLA. Director, Ataxia Center and HD Center of Excellence. 300 UCLA Med Plaza, Suite B200 Los Angeles.

I remember at a Bible study, when we had to introduce ourselves with one word using the first letter of our first name, mine being "A", I said "Adaptable", which has been very appropriate in the circumstances.

My Christian faith has and does really help me to cope with the changes. God gives me the strength to cope with this. I have met or heard of people who wanted to commit suicide, or fell into a depressed state, or took to their bed for months because of their diagnosis and what the outcome usually is for them.

I don't know how I would have dealt with ataxia had it not been for my Christian faith. I don't want ataxia, but I've got it.

I've learnt new moves as well, the chicken dance being one of them. This happens when I'm usually cutting food or I flap about like a chicken when I'm falling, you know you're going and there's nothing you can do about it.

If I didn't have ataxia I would not have been able to write this book, now there's a positive!

Ataxia

This chapter on ataxia is to give people a little understanding of what ataxia is and what it can do to people, <u>but I can only say what ataxia has done to me</u>. It can affect everyone who has ataxia differently and usually at different rates. People who have ataxia will most likely have heard all this. This is for people who probably haven't even heard of the word, let alone know what ataxia is. I was one of those people and still am (and still scratch my head about it).

Ataxia can be a result of having various neurological and medical conditions, i.e. multiple sclerosis (MS), spinocerebellar atrophy (SCA), stroke, head trauma, brain tumor, peripheral neuropathy, to name but a very few.

Ataxia affects the cells in the cerebellum; that is the part of the brain that controls your gait (being able to walk) and motor skills (buttoning things, writing etc.). The cerebellum is at the bottom part of the head. The left part of the cerebellum controls the left side of the body, and the right part controls the right side of the body.

I will try to explain a little bit about ataxia the best I can, but if you (family members, friends, care-givers, etc.) want to find out more about ataxia, the NAF (National Ataxia Foundation) is an excellent source of information for anyone who has been affected by ataxia or has an interest in it. The following has been taken from the NAF site, hopefully this is easier to understand than me trying to explain ataxia to you and making it as clear as mud.

> [2]*The word ataxia means without coordination. People with ataxia have problems with coordination because parts of the nervous system that control movement and balance are affected. Ataxia may affect the fingers, hands, arms, legs, body, speech, and eye movements.*
>
> *There is a large group of people who have symptoms of ataxia that usually begin in adulthood and who have no known family history of this disease. This is called sporadic ataxia and it can be difficult to diagnose. There are many acquired and hereditary causes of ataxia which must be ruled out before a diagnosis of sporadic ataxia can be made. Sporadic ataxia can be either "pure cerebellar" if only the cerebellum is affected or cerebellar plus, if the ataxia is accompanied by additional symptoms such a neuropathy (dysfunction of the peripheral nerves); dementia (impaired intellectual function); or weakness, rigidity, or spasticity of the muscles.*

Disability may be greater and progress more quickly with the cerebellar plus form of sporadic ataxia. The cerebellar plus form of sporadic ataxia is also known as sporadic Olivopontocerebellar ataxia sporadic (OPCA) or multiple system atrophy, cerebellar type (MSA-C).

Sporadic ataxia is a term designating a group of diseases of the central nervous system that occur without evidence that they are inherited, that is, no other person in the affected individual's family has ever had the same disorder.

Physicians in the past have used various terms when they made a diagnosis of sporadic ataxia. Some of these terms include: • Olivopontocerebellar atrophy (OPCA) or Olivopontocerebellar degeneration • Idiopathic late onset cerebellar atrophy or degeneration (ILOCA or ILOCD).

(National Ataxia Foundation)

Apparently mine is sporadic ataxia. To my knowledge, no-one in my family from my father's or mother's side has had anything similar at all.

---

[2] Paragraphs in italics have been taken, with their permission, from the NAF (National Ataxia Foundation) website. Paragraphs in bold print were kindly supplied by Dr Susan L Perlman.

Having ataxia isn't a death sentence. It has taught me to be more patient, and besides I've got no choice. You can spend more energy having a hissy fit than just doing whatever needs to be done, or delegating if it's something you simply can't do. It can take longer to do most things, i.e. one of the things for me is getting out or putting back the milk jug in the fridge. Whereas before I could do it in a straight line as the crow flies, now the milk jug is taken the long way, via the sink, worktops and the stove, using them as support with one hand while gripping the milk jug (which now only gets half-filled at a time, with less chance of me spilling it). Sometimes it is done in stages, put the milk jug down, walk a bit with walker, pick the jug back up, and put it back down again, as you can imagine it's a process. Something that used to take me a few seconds now takes me a few minutes.

Do what you can, or learn how to do things in a different way. I have a bungee cord attached to the laundry basket so I can at least pull the laundry basket, but I have to be aware not to look back and then forward quickly (unlike I used to be able to do). I found out the hard way — I ended up sitting in the basket which ended up sideways, and no idea how that happened. At least half of me had enjoyed a comfy landing, and I just missed the cat's dishes which I had filled up only minutes before. I have attached a bungee to the door handle so I can close the door after myself; It is safer me than having to back-track in order to pull the door closed behind me.

I do stuff that I shouldn't do and I can tell if it wears me out. I was told by my OT (Occupational Therapist) a few years ago, "Conserve your energy." Now I can understand why. It's a bitter pill to swallow, accepting that finding a way to do things is now different. It does take longer to do things, or there might be something you just can't do now. One of the things for me is walking — just being able to get up and go anywhere without having to think about doing it. I still think I am okay to do something while I'm sitting down, but then realization hits you once you get up.

Now for the fun part, the genes — talk about muddy waters.

What is the difference between hereditary and genetic, and there is a difference. Hereditary can be passed on genetically to one's offspring. Genetic is to do with the genes.

Some terms you might have heard of and a short meaning of those terms are:

Autosomal — male or female can be affected.

Dominantly inherited is a condition passed down to each child from a parent that has the condition and each child has a 50% chance of developing the condition.

How an Autosomal Dominant
Disorder is Passed on in a Family

Father with one **A** and one
a (has ataxia)

Mother with two **a**'s (does
not have ataxia)

A = disease gene
a = normal gene

When a parent with autosomal dominant ataxia and
a parent without ataxia produce offspring, each of the
offspring will either inherit ataxia or not inherit ataxia
depending on which genes are passed on.

Offspring who inherit one
ataxia-causing gene will
have ataxia.

Offspring who inherit two
normal genes will not have
ataxia.

Courtesy of National Ataxia Foundation fact sheet:

"Understanding Genetics"

i.e. Spinocerebellar atrophy (SCA) is a dominantly inherited condition.

Recessive ataxia is hereditary that is in the genes but can lie dormant for generations then can affect a person.

How an Autosomal Recessive
Disorder is Passed on in a Family

Father with one **F** and one **f**
(does not have ataxia)

Mother with one **f** and one **F**
(does not have ataxia)

F = normal gene
f = disease gene

The above parents each have one recessive ataxia-causing gene. Each of their offspring could inherit one of four possible gene combinations:

F from father, **f** from mother
(child does not have ataxia
but can pass disease gene on
to future children)

f from father, **F** from mother
(child does not have ataxia
but can pass disease gene on
to future children)

F from father, **F** from mother
(child does not have ataxia and
has no disease gene to pass on
to future children)

f from father, **f** from mother
(double-dose of ataxia-causing
gene means child will have
ataxia and will pass disease
gene on to all future children)

Courtesy of National Ataxia Foundation fact sheet:

"Understanding Genetics"

i.e. Fredreich's Ataxia is a recessively inherited condition.

Recessive <u>ataxias</u> require two bad genes (one from the father and one from the mother) to cause ataxia. A family can carry one bad gene

for generations with no one developing ataxia. However if someone marries into the family who also carries that same bad gene, then their children could develop ataxia.

(Dr S Perlman)

Diagnosis is based on a person's medical history, family history, and a complete neurological evaluation including an MRI scan of the brain. Various blood tests may be performed to rule out other possible disorders which may present similar symptoms. Genetic blood tests are now available for some types of hereditary ataxia to confirm a diagnosis or as a predictive test to determine if someone has inherited an ataxia gene known to affect other family members.

Both scientific and medical research is on going in the United States and many other countries to determine the cause of ataxia and devise better methods to diagnose and to treat the ataxias. The research includes both the hereditary and the sporadic forms of ataxia.

(National Ataxia Foundation)

At this time as far as I know there is no cure or treatment for ataxia, and there is no remission; once it starts it's like a snowball, it just keeps on going. This is known as the "progression" of the condition.

One thing I have gotten to realize is that ataxia is only the outcome of something else. I realized this on reading online about how some people can have ataxia and still swim, go to a gym or walk a distance (with or without a rollator).

Muscle weakness is my biggest issue. I can eventually get down, usually by getting on my knees, but then I can have problems getting back up. I crawl on my hands and knees to something that I can feel secure enough about pulling myself up on, i.e. sofa, bed, between door frames (like Samson did with the two pillars). If that fails and I am truly stuck getting upright, I holler; David hears me, and has to pull me up.

It's like the feeling you have when you're recovering from a bout of 'flu, when you feel okay but your body gets tired after you have do something i.e. take the rubbish out, walk up the stairs or mow the lawn or whatever. Even though you felt like you were okay to do it, so you did, but then you feel worn out even if you hardly did anything. Also imagine hands that have been placed in cold water or sit on them for a few minutes, they're pretty numb after doing either. Now try to do something with them, like fastening a button, writing your name, turning a page of a book; it feels awkward, you know how and what to do but your body can't. It can be frustrating.

The NAF are doing an ataxia spin challenge; you sit on a chair and spin around until you're dizzy, then get off the chair and try to walk holding a cup of water. It gives a person an idea of what it is like for someone with ataxia. I cried when I first saw it and it still upsets me, seeing a person who can walk normally like I used to, then making themselves dizzy, but then able to go back to walking normally again. But I think at the same time: what a brilliant example of giving a person an idea of what it feels like, trying to walk while doing something else at the same time.

I used to be able to walk normally and was able to carry a cup of tea no problem, but now I live with this ataxia. You can't put it down and then pick it back up; people can't walk away from ataxia, they can sympathize with you, but people can leave it when they have to go. People live with ataxia day in and day out. You can't take a pill one night, then the next morning wake up and be back to the way you were before ataxia happened. Unless your ataxia can be helped with drugs or therapy.

Olivopontocerebellar atrophy (OPCA)

OPCA is an MRI diagnosis of atrophy of the olives (brainstem), pons and cerebellum. If someone does not have an MRI that looks like that, then they can't be called OPCA.

(Dr S Perlman)

This is a description that explains what an MRI is:

Magnetic resonance imaging (MRI) is a non-invasive medical test that helps physicians diagnose and treat medical conditions.

If a contrast material will be used in the MRI exam, a physician, nurse or technologist will insert an intravenous (IV) catheter, also known as an IV line, into a vein in your hand or arm. A saline solution may be used. The solution will drip through the IV to prevent blockage of the IV catheter until the contrast material is injected.

> Detailed MR images allow physicians to evaluate various parts of the body and determine the presence of certain diseases.
>
> (Radiologyinfo.org)

I had the OPCA diagnosis which showed that when the MRI was examined by a neurologist it indicated deterioration of my part of the brain that is to do with the motor skills, the olives, the pons and the cerebellum (OPCA). It is a degenerative condition, it can progress slowly or progress quickly. From what I have been told, mine is progressing slowly

MSA (Multiple System Atrophy)

Sporadic ataxia often later develops Parkinsonian symptoms of slowness and stiffness of movement along with difficulty turning over in bed and rising from a soft chair ...

(National Ataxia Foundation)

I can attest to those two things definitely as that did and does now happen to me a lot. A year ago when we were staying in another State overnight, David went to feed and water the sheep. I saw a really comfy looking wing-backed chair. I always liked that type of chair. I sat in it, but when I tried to get off the chair I couldn't, as much as I tried. It was a rocker; it didn't just rock back and forth but it was a swivel chair too. Every time I tried to get out moved, it either rocked back and forth or swiveled around— well I was stuck in it for about 30 minutes until David came back and had to haul me out of it.

It's a struggle getting into bed and turning, I'd do well with a rope to help me move easier. Talk about flopping into bed and hoping I don't fall out. One time I did this, I misjudged and ended up on the floor. My next step that seems to be the way I may have to go is getting bed safety rails. I have been looking at them so at least when I do get into bed I won't be falling out, as now it's even a struggle actually getting on to the bed and then attempting to turn. I never thought that could be so exhausting in itself. I have always liked to wrap the bedding around me, makes me feel more secure. Like a little sausage roll.

This MSA sure makes one think, as if ataxia didn't already do that.

MSA-C or MSA-P is based on what is primarily predominant ie:

MSA-C primarily the <u>cerebellum</u> is affected

MSA-P has primary characteristics similar to <u>Parkinson's</u> disease

Research into MSA is very active now.

One of the many emails I sent to Dr Perlman as I was so confused about all these names and what was what? Her answer made so much sense to me. I hope it makes sense to you too.

Hello Dr Perlman

More questions.

Is MSA the same as sporadic ataxia? I thought sporadic ataxia developed into MSA, I had never heard of MSA until a few months ago. I have read it's just another name for sporadic ataxia. Does it mean it was always MSA but was called OPCA?

Thank you again

Angela MacLauchlan

20-25% of patients developing sporadic ataxia will progress to MSA, which involves the cerebellum and the basal ganglia and the autonomic nervous system (hence, multiple system atrophy).

OPCA was the first name given to non-genetic ataxia. It has been replaced by sporadic ataxia or "idiopathic late onset cerebellar ataxia", as not all patients have the MRI features of OPCA (some may just have cerebellar atrophy, rather than <u>O</u>livo<u>P</u>onto<u>C</u>erebellar <u>A</u>trophy).

(Dr S Perlman)

MSA is a rare, degenerative neurological condition that affects both men and women, usually starting in their 50s or early 60s.

The condition was first identified in 1962 and named Shy-Drager syndrome after the names of the two physicians who reported patients showing a combination of Parkinson's-like movement disorders, and problems with the autonomic, or body-regulating division of the nervous system. See more at:

https://www.multiplesystematrophy.org/about-msa#sthash.h5MOgVww.dpuf

It is not inherited and it is not contagious.
(MSA Coalition website)

This condition was identified in the year I was born!!!!

According to the NAF website, sporadic ataxia affects 1 in 100,000 people. MSA affects 4 in 100,000 but included in this number are the people who usually have developed Parkinson's symptoms and then autonomic failure, but have not experienced ataxia.

I feel honoured to have such a rare condition. I would do cartwheels along the street if I could, but I can't, probably would be carted away to some place if I did anyway.

Some people might think I find this all as one big joke; I don't intend to be flippant, I have to make the best of this situation. God gave me a positive attitude, I have to look at the positives. I am not going to lie down and cry; that wouldn't help me, and the condition would probably progress more quickly too.

With MSA, we can lose our ability to do things at a rate of 25-30% each year, compared to someone with Parkinson's who usually loses the ability to do things at a rate of 1-2% each year. Parkinson's is another horrible condition to have as well. Ataxia is a movement disorder and usually has similar conditions, but a lot more people have heard of Parkinson's, while very few people have heard of ataxia.

Losing the ability to do things no matter at what rate is devastating to that individual. If I was honest, the lifespan is not good for someone with MSA. A medical textbook, doctor or a neurologist might give us a time factor but they can only roughly estimate according to past clients.

Only God knows when our time is up, and when that time is up, it's up, wherever we are. I do hope to achieve reaching my 60th birthday, and to be aware that it is. As I said before, only God knows that time. He has His reasons for me having this, I don't understand why, but He does. The outcome is not at all appealing, I am sure a lot of people would agree with that, and so being negative wouldn't help any of us, would it? All the tears and tantrums won't make it go away.

Early Signs

1996 - 2009

In 1996 I was 34 years old; which is when I started to experience my first symptom, not knowing at the time what it was. I went to my doctor with numbness in the right side of my chin. It felt like when you go to the dentist and they give you an injection that freezes your mouth i.e. for a filling. When the injection starts to wear off — there's that numb feeling — you can feel the outside of your skin on your face but nothing under the skin. I was sent to the dental hospital as they thought it was something to do with my teeth. My teeth/gums were found not to be causing the problem.

After a few visits I was sent for an MRI. The MRI result was clear, it showed nothing. The numbness to this day is still there and now it is also in the left side of my chin; nothing major, I have gotten so used to it that it doesn't concern me.

I've never had strength in my hands, even as a kid; I wouldn't have made a professional arm wrestler. I couldn't even ride a bike, unless of course one had stabilizers attached to the back wheels, in which case I may have been able to ride it.

I always seemed to have problems with trying to keep my balance on anything that had only two wheels or just two blades such as ice skates. I could balance okay on roller skates because they had four wheels.

My legs — now that was different — they were where my strength was. I used to walk everywhere regardless of the distance. I liked walking and running. I did notice however, I always had a problem keeping flip-flop type of shoes on, with my left foot especially.

When I was a smoker a few years ago (I have since given up that habit, thankfully) the cigarette would suddenly 'ping' out of my left hand fingers. A bit like when you're holding chopsticks and they keep crossing because you're having problems using them. Pens and pencils would suddenly 'ping' out of my fingers for no reason.

When I used to cut my son's hair about 15 years ago, my left hand would cramp when holding the hair between my fingers while cutting it. Again, the fingers of the left hand. I had no problem knitting though. I don't do knitting enough, and have since learnt its good exercise for the hand.

Over the years I went to the doctor with various problems resulting from having this condition, but not being aware of having ataxia. I thought all my symptoms were problems of their own. The numbness I had, plus a funny feeling like rushing water through my left wrist, and a tingling in my left wrist. One symptom must have made my doctor think that I'd lost the plot — my head felt too heavy for my neck. I would sit with my hand under my chin holding my head up.

According to my mum I would trip going up the stairs (this would be in the early 90s). Objects 'pinging' out of my hand, and the cramps, I didn't even mention to a doctor. I felt like a hypochondriac.

Over the years when I went to the doctor for something I was experiencing to do with this condition, it felt very real to me, but because the condition was in the early stages and didn't rear its ugly head until later, nothing wrong was ever found. But put all the things I was experiencing together (a bit like joining up the dots) and then the condition causing the issues I experienced over the years wasn't actually diagnosed until 2009.

About 2002 I noticed that I couldn't lift my left foot very well; it seemed heavy and to slap down when I walked; it felt like I was wearing a wooden shoe. This went on for quite a few months. I then started to trip up because I was unable to lift my foot up when I walked. I also noticed that if my hair got in my face (more noticeably if it was windy) and covered my eyes, that I would trip up.

One Friday after I finished work I was on my way to get the bus. I saw the bus arriving, so I ran for it but fell flat on my face; everyone on the bus must have seen it. Needless to say I missed the bus. I blamed it on my foot getting caught in the legs of my trousers.

Exactly a week later on the following Friday after work, I walked along on the path beside the main road to catch the bus home. No way was I going to run for it, not after my fall the week before, but I then ended up on the ground again, and this was while I was only just walking! I tripped up and put a hole in the knee of my trousers, something I hadn't done since I was a kid.

I found it hard to believe that at my age I had put a hole in the knee of my trousers, how embarrassing; honestly, to me that was the worst part. When I told my friend she said I should get this checked out in case it was something serious. This was when I finally made my first appointment to see my general doctor regarding this, by now it was early 2004.

I told the doctor that I had fallen in about 2000 - 2001 and that my left knee took the fall. Also the same year, I started work as a security guard and would travel on the overnight bus to our destination. On one of these journeys my legs were bent up against the seat in front of me all night, and in the morning I remember my left knee feeling painful when I woke up, as it had been in that position all night. That's the only two things I could think of to explain why I was experiencing these problems.

Also by this time my balance was starting to cause me concern. I found it difficult to walk straight if the space in front of me was blocked, or while walking at a slow pace that would cause me problems I would lose my balance. The doctor asked if I drank alcohol, as the symptoms I was experiencing were similar to someone with a drinking problem. I didn't have that problem as I didn't drink alcohol, only hot tea with milk and sugar.

The doctor made an appointment for me to see a podiatrist. After examining me, the podiatrist said she couldn't explain what the problem was and it wasn't anything that her profession would be able to help me with. She did say that my bum was losing muscle, and my shoulder was drooping, and that I was a medical mystery. She was really nice, and as helpful as she could be. Still no answers to what was causing my problems though.

Back off to the general doctor, and it's now May 2006. The doctor took blood tests. I was also wee-ing more frequently. My B12 level was 95 and I was anemic, but a diabetes test was negative. I got a prescription for B12 tablets and folic acid tablets and was to take them for 2-3 months. Then I went back for repeat blood tests, and my B12 level was now about 160. With taking the B12 tablets I did notice an improvement.

At work in the office and sitting down, after a while the backs of my thighs would start to feel uncomfortable, sort of achy, but never painful. Taking the B12 tablet helped this achy feeling to go away. Even though I did improve, I was still walking like I was under the influence of something. The doctor then referred me to a neurologist.

In July 2006 I went to see Neurologist Number One, who was in Scotland. He tested my B12 levels and tested me for other things, diabetes being one of them (it seemed to be the most common thing everyone thought was the cause, because of my symptoms). He did various other tests in his office that day that I didn't do that well on — balance being one — you had to walk in baby steps, heel to toe. I failed that one big-time, I could only do about two steps, and by then I was swaying all over the place. Next, stand in one place with your arms stretched out — failed that one too — I couldn't do it.

He gave me a brace to help prevent me tripping up, which worked fine for that, but made my balance worse. You could only wear flat lace-up shoes with the brace, but at least you could walk without tripping over your foot. By then I couldn't walk wearing flat shoes or I'd walk like I was drunk, or I could walk okay without the brace and risk falling flat on my face. What's your preference, walk like you're drunk, or kiss the pavement.

Neurologist Number One then sent me for an MRI. I was getting tested for multiple sclerosis, but I didn't know that as the neurologist decided not to tell me; he must have thought I'd freak out in his office. Having a balance issue and running about freaking out don't go together, unless I was going about on my hands and knees, then I wouldn't risk tripping up.

The MRI result was fine and nothing to be concerned about. Then I had the electrical test, people will probably know it better as the "shocks and pin-pricks test" — this is what I call it. This is done by the neurologist. Little needles are inserted into your muscles; that's bearable, it really is okay. Then shocks are made to those little needles while they are still stuck in your muscles. The readings are then read by the neurologist. It's like someone has a tuning fork, gets it to hum by hitting it on something, then zaps your muscles with it — not so bearable then. I was glad when that test was done. It only takes about 30 minutes in total.

The result of that test when I went back to see him for the follow-up, was that I had peripheral neuropathy. He told me to keep on taking the B12 tablets, and come back and see him in 3 months. I didn't get to go back as by then I was in the USA.

I went to see Neurologist Number Two here in the US in March or May 2007. According to this gentleman I didn't even have peripheral neuropathy or a balance problem; it was an injury to my knee that was making me walk weirdly. I went for about 10 months thinking it was just my age causing the problems I was experiencing, because of what Neurologist Number Two had said to me.

A few months after visiting Neurologist Number Two, I had just gotten off the phone to my aunt, and when I stood up my balance was off. Trying to regain it, I tripped and went full-speed over the living room floor into the TV and a table with a plant sitting on it. The plant that was on the table didn't get damaged one bit, but I on the other hand damaged my left foot. I had to get an X-ray; I really thought I had broken or fractured it, but the X-ray showed it was okay.

A few months later it was still painful so I went to a podiatrist who X-rayed it and showed my foot was okay. I explained what was happening with my balance etc. and what Neurologist Number Two had said. The podiatrist suggested I get things checked out again. I was concerned that this balance and weird walking was not an "age thing" and that I was not imagining it. I was only in my early 40s and no-one else seemed to have this problem at my age, or older.

So back I went to the general doctor; I wanted to see about this balance issue and get it fixed. Neurologist Number

Two had sent a letter to my doctor saying my balance was fine. He really hadn't listened to what I'd said. I got another referral to a different neurologist.

In June - July 2008 I went to see Neurologist Number Three, as my balance had got worse and I still couldn't lift my left foot; I also couldn't walk very well if it was dark. Any sudden change of direction in my movements left or right, and my balance got worse. I would be walking straight ahead, and if I took a sudden right turn, my brain was still going straight, while my body was going right and it would throw me off-balance, until of course my brain had figured out the way I was going, until I changed direction again. So any sudden change of direction, and I was banging into the wall.

Neurologist Number Three did that pin-prick and shock test. The result was I had peripheral neuropathy. He explained what it was, and was asking questions, like did I have problems walking in crowds or in the dark. He was saying to me the same things as Neurologist Number One had said to me.

I have to admit it was a relief, hearing all that Neurologist Number Three was saying the same as Neurologist Number One had said, that it was peripheral neuropathy; it wasn't my age or any knee injury causing this. I was told to keep taking my B12 tablets and come back if there were any changes.

In November 2008 when I was walking I noticed that after walking about 20 minutes my right leg felt weird. It felt like a tube; I could feel the outside but felt like there was nothing but jelly inside the leg. If I had needed to walk any further I would not have been able to. The leg went back to normal after I sat down. It happened again a few weeks later, after walking about 20-30 minutes.

In December 2008 - January 2009 I trotted back off to Neurologist Number Three. He sent me for a spinal MRI. The result was that everything was okay. He examined me and wanted me to go to the Mayo Clinic for a second opinion. This symptom regarding my right leg was nothing to do with the peripheral neuropathy. It did feel like a different sensation to what my left leg would feel. My left leg had never felt like this at any time.

The hospital here in town couldn't help me, and said I should go to the Mayo. The health insurance company said the Mayo was too far way, and suggested the University of Colorado Hospital.

July 2009 I started getting twitching in my legs and arms. It didn't make my limbs jerk, just twitching feelings inside, like a fluttering feeling. If one has had a baby, it's like a baby moving inside your stomach. If one hasn't had a baby, best way I can explain it would be like a little man inside your muscle, lightly tapping at it.

My husband and I went to University of Colorado Hospital in September 2009 and saw Neurologist Number Four who did the shock and pin-prick test. She then sent me for an MRI where they put an IV in your arm so that the dye shows up things in your brain. Neurologist Number Four called me a few weeks later to tell me the MRI showed shrinkage of the brain, on the side to do with co-ordination and motor skills, which explained the imbalance and dropping things etc.

I have a condition that is called Olivopontocerebellar atrophy (its posh name) or OPCA for short. There is no treatment or cure for it; just eat healthy, get plenty of rest and exercise — general advice everyone gets for everything. Genetic blood tests were arranged. The results of the blood tests were negative for SCA1 and SCA 2, and it was not hereditary. One of my genes might have gone wrong.

Later I called back to see what I do now, do I have to have an annual check-up etc. Neurologist Number Four said to contact the MDA clinic where I live, or I was welcome to come back to Colorado. At that time the MDA (Muscular Dystrophy Association) clinic said they don't deal with my type of condition as it comes under hereditary neurology. Brick wall time!

It's like you have this condition, and it's rare; no- one really knows anything about it; there's no cure, no treatment; now you're on your own. I have questions and I'm not really sure what I have, let alone know what this "OPCA" is. No-one seems to know much about ataxia. I have no idea what or where to turn to find out anything about it. What number of SCA do I have, if this even has a number? Is ataxia hereditary? How long before I'm unable to do <u>anything</u>? What's my outcome? To name but a few questions!

One of the first things I did when I had a name to this condition was to go on to the internet. There was not a lot online about ataxia at that time, unlike all the information that we can find nowadays. I found a relevant video, but after watching it I really thought I had about two weeks to live, with me eventually choking to death. It was a big mistake going on to the internet, I still remember sights from that video; I don't think I will ever forget them. It was abit far-fetched, but it was all the "facts" I could find at that time.

I called Neurologist Number Three to see where I could go or what to do next. They told me they would try the hospital here again, to see if they could do anything for me without having to return to Colorado.

Now I am on to Neurologist Number Five. Since my Colorado visit they now have a neurologist here in my town that I can go and see.

Then in November - December 2009 the fingers on my left hand changed. They wouldn't go together on their own; I have to push them together, and they won't straighten outwards, they want to curl inwards like you do when you clench your hand.

The twitching in my arms and legs is a lot less frequent than it used to be; just an odd twitch now and then, and the twitching of my right eye has stopped. My eyesight has gotten worse but I don't know if it's my neurological condition, or old age. Having a good light and larger print to read helps a lot. .

At evening time, mostly then, I get to a stage where I have to lie down; like the levels in me have to level off. Imagine a test tube bottle half full of liquid, then you turn it on its side so the liquid in the bottle levels off. That's the easiest way to explain what it feels like.

If I don't take my B12 tablets, after a couple of days my legs, especially in my thighs, start to get that achy feeling but it goes away by the next day if I take B12 tablets again.

I do still have to go for a wee more often than I used to. If I go down a hill or a ramp it can put me off-balance; my head is still level with the pavement even though my body isn't. Heat affects me; I can only do something in it for about 5 minutes. Imagine a flower standing up all perky, then after a few days of not being watered, it starts to droop and wilt; that's exactly what it feels like being in the heat. I have to lie down, or sit with my feet up and have the fan blowing on me. After about 10 minutes I feel better and then I can go back into the heat until I feel like I am wilting again. When I'm tired I bang into things or trip up more often than usual.

Of all these symptoms I have had, thankfully none has ever been painful.

I remember the days when I could multi-task; I could walk, talk and text all at the same time. I tried to put a top on and was walking at the same time, the sleeve blocked my view and I tripped. I learned not to do that again. Multi-tasking nowadays — forget it!

Anyway it's better to concentrate on one thing at a time, and less stressful too. My right hand seems to be starting to change too. I noticed my toes on the right foot wanting to turn downwards towards the floor.

My inquiry letter to a doctor in Colorado

PO Box 9081
Albuquerque
NM, 87119
28 September 09

Dear Doctor ....

Thank you for calling me on Friday. It is now Monday and I have so many questions going on inside my head. I have looked on the internet and it seems to be giving me more questions. I hope you wouldn't mind answering them, or what you can answer for me.

1. Is it definitely opca, is there any chance it could be something else?
2. Does it make a difference what type of opca, how do find that out?
3. What can I do to slow down progression, certain foods, any medicine, and exercise can make a difference. Does heat make it progress quicker?
4. Have I still got peripheral neuropathy and this is a branch of it or is this totally different thing?

5. Am I having blood drawn just to see if I have the heredity gene?

6. Do I still need to take B12 pills, will it be checked to see if I have a deficiency?

7. When would my onset of opca have started?

8. Did it not show up anything on my last MRI?

9. My speech, tired, legs and arms ache after a while of use, I just started noticing this last year, does this mean it's fast progressing?

10. How long will I be able to live normal, i.e. dress and be able to feed myself, be mobile? How many years roughly, can you tell by the shrinkage of my brain?

11. Do I need to go to a neurologist or doctor here to see how it's progressing?

I know it's a lot of questions but I don't know what to do or where to go for information. Do you know of any self-help groups?

It would be really appreciated if you do get a chance to answer my questions, I apologize for there being so many, and you could email me if that's easier.

My First Set of Wheels

2012

Got my very own set of wheels today; a pretty blue they are and they are free to run. But all I have done with them is wheel them out to the car; they are pretty to look at and that's all I have done, just admired them; it's a walker — not for me surely. Why do I need a walker, I have a forearm crutch and am getting used to that, and now there's been an upgrade. If I were honest, I'd admit to needing it, because now it seems like walking for more than 5 minutes is too much and I need to take a seat. This walker has got a seat; you can push down on the handles or sit down on the seat, and the brakes go on, so hopefully I won't be doing any wheelies with it.

I am thankful for the walker; it gives me more independence. There's a basket under the seat for a bag, and when you are in a shop you can put the shopping basket on the seat so you're not having to depend on other people to carry things for you, and you can sit down whenever you need to. I have seen people in restaurants put their food tray on the seat and push it around. Now that might be a bit adventurous for me just now, but a bit more experience under my belt and whey-hay, no problem!

How did one get about before walkers; in the films you'd see people stuck in basket chairs. Thank God for small mercies. The thought of being plopped in a basket chair year-round doesn't sound appealing to me. Crutches, I imagined they used big sticks as a way of getting about, but if they got tired and wanted to sit, did they have to sit down on the ground or were they house-bound because they could not get out as they used to. They did not have anything to help them to get about; thank God for small mercies.

My wheels are no cost to use, user-friendly and you can stop, put the brakes on and sit down whenever you have to. I'm thinking of putting a horn on to warn people that there is a person coming up behind. Nah, probably not a good idea; it'd give people a fright, then they might want to sue me as they dropped their favourite cup and it broke because I'd given them a fright by honking my horn.

My people stick (crutch) has ribbon on it. So I will decorate the walker too. Make the most of it; you have got a walker whether you want it or not. Think of it as something you have to put on to go out, like your shoes, usually you put them on to go out; most people wouldn't go out without footwear on their feet.

My Second Set of Wheels

2015

Now it's been three years since my first-ever walker, which I now don't use. It was at the stage that when I pressed down on the handles to put the brakes on, the walker would still keep moving along. So now it didn't work for me, and a few times I felt it moving away from me when I tried to sit down on it, so it was no longer a safe thing for me to use. The walker itself wasn't the problem; I just didn't have enough strength to put the brakes on. Because of the ataxia I also walk with my feet further apart, so I kept kicking the wheels and tripping up over them.

I now have one that probably almost everyone has seen around, sometimes called a "zimmer frame". It has two tennis balls on the back frame at the bottom to make it glide easier, and it has two stationary wheels at the front. I had them changed to the plastic sliders which are made for walkers, instead of using the tennis balls. The sliders are a lot easier to put on the walker, and the sliders make the walker glide more easily, mind you the walker glides too easily for my liking. I will go back to using the tennis balls again eventually. I can make the walker pivot easier when I turn a corner too with the tennis balls on.

I find the zimmer frame safer to use, as it moves when I want it to, unlike the other walker, because that had universal wheels at the front; it was too free-motion for me.

This walker (the zimmer frame one) is also a lot easier to fold and put in the car, even I can manage to do that. You can get one that has a lighter frame, but I find them too flimsy for me; I like the heavier framed ones, they're much sturdier. I do miss the basket and seat of my older walker, but I sewed a pouch for my newest walker; a kangaroo has a pouch and now so do I. It's like having a bag — you can keep your phone, purse, tissues, glasses etc. in it, and I have a plastic hook attached on the front bar for my handbag if I want to take one.

Some pouches I made for my walker

I bought a universal tray that slips over the handles, for carrying items like a computer or even the laundry, but you have to remember you are pushing the walker, so you don't overload the tray with things. I use it mostly for transporting my cups of tea or coffee. I put a piece of kitchen towel on the tray, so the towel is a guide if am walking too fast with my walker, like I don't go slow enough as it is. I put my cup of liquid on the towel, cover the cup with a plastic lid or coaster, and push the walker very slowly to where I will be sitting. I need to do this, as walking while carrying something is now a no-no for me. The universal tray doesn't involve much strength so it works for me. I am able to put the tray on myself without the need to ask someone to do it for me.

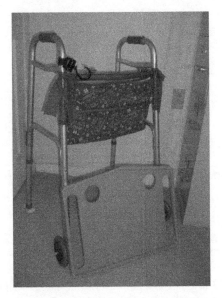

The removable tray for my walker

I have a little flashlight that clips onto the front of the frame of the walker, I call it my "headlight"; it lights up just enough to show a beam of light. It helps when I have to walk in the dark, usually going to the toilet in the middle of the night.

Power Chair

2015

I got my first electric power chair about three years ago, a nice red one and it turns around so it can be used in small places, as opposed to an electric scooter which would be pretty difficult to turn in small places. My hall is only about 4ft wide so my power chair works well for me.

My chair has five little dots on the joy stick that light up to let you know how much charge it has left. It also has a horn button and a START and a STOP button. There is a lever on the seat that I can use to raise and lower the back-rest. The arms lift up. I have a cushion to sit on as the seat is hard. I would recommend a good cushion so it lasts and doesn't get that flat feeling (like some pillows get) and then it's not as comfortable to sit on. They can be expensive but so worth it in the long-run. Mine was a few hundred dollars but it has lasted about three years; I had a cheaper one and it only lasted after sitting on it only a few times. It now stays in the car and I use it for the manual chair and it works for that, but I don't use it that often.

I took the cover off the cushion to wash it and couldn't get the cover back on, so now I just use a pillow-case and am forever changing that. You could make your cushion cover and a pouch to match. Now there's a sewing project in the making! I do need a pouch for my chair to carry the phone, glasses etc. about, just like the pouch I have on my walker. It seems even trying to carry something in my hand or on my thighs while driving my power chair is multi-tasking for me, and that's not a good idea.

The power chair looks easy to use, until you have to use it. Any appliances we have now have dents in them, never mind that previously they didn't, now they look all beat up — compliments of my driving skills.

The arms of mine match the paint on the inside walls of the house. The walls in the hallway and the doorframes right now are cream colored with putty colored stripes on the walls and frames. We had someone putty up the holes in the walls and doorframes, and I must be getting better as there are less holes in the wall now than before. Practice those power chair driving skills! I have to use the electric power chair more often now than I used to.

You need a lift on your vehicle for the electric power chair so the chair can be transported; we do have one, a manual lift, where you have to wheel the power chair on to the lift by way of the lift ramp and then strap it down. This can take about 15-20 minutes to do. I have seen lifts that are operated by a switch in the car, which then lifts the power chair into the back of your vehicle for you, a lot easier to operate. This is a goal for me, something that I can do myself; what a goal, I never thought that would be something I would want, let alone think I would need.

A manual wheelchair is handy as it can be folded up and can be carried in most car boots (trunks). This is ideal, as you don't have to take a special vehicle, and if the other person is okay pushing you around in the manual wheelchair, you can go most places. Before you and your helper go out, do check how the wheelchair folds up. If you don't use it often, it's surprising what a puzzle it turns out to be. I was in this situation once, talk about feeling dumb, not knowing how to fold my own wheelchair. Another lesson learnt the hard way.

One of my issues that I have with a manual chair is that someone has to push me; due to weakness in my arms I can't maneuver it for more than a few minutes, if that. Now using my feet I can go for longer, backwards though, which is really handy; at least I have been able to move without someone's help, but that's me just being me.

Give me an electric chair and I'm off; I could travel miles if I had someone else in a chair to go with. One thing you have to remember to do is charge it up, just like a phone. The more you use it the more often you have to charge it, and mine has colored lights that let me know when it's running low. The faster you make it go, the more energy it uses.

Having a power chair has limited me going to places that I used to like going to; flea-markets, yard sales, most Goodwill stores and shopping malls. A lot of places are just not set up for power chairs, and it wouldn't be a safe environment for the other people or me. But if you really want to go somewhere, that's where the manual chair does come in handy. If a baby buggy can get there then a manual chair probably can to. It takes away the stress of driving, but it can be frustrating as you can't just go at the drop of a hat when you want to.

The Trouble with Tuppence

As soon as I sit in my power chair now, Tuppence the cat runs away — he's probably sick of getting run over. Honestly, I have looked behind me the best I can before I reverse, but where do you think he chooses to lie —, snuggled up asleep right behind me so I can't see him. Thinking its okay, I reverse but then I hear him shrieking, then he bolts leaving a big clump of fur on the floor, presumably from his tail. I thought cats were meant to be clever. The horn has no effect on him at all; it's not loud, so I usually have to say "move" and he moves out of my way, usually.

Now the cat is back and has taken to sitting on the seat of my power chair; and it seems to be a race who is going get there first, me or him. So now he is probably fed up with getting shoved off the seat of my chair so he starts to sit on the foot-rest. Out of the bathroom I come and there he is, sitting on the foot-rest. He can stay there while I move the chair and take him for a little ride.

So off we go, or so I think, then there is another almighty cat screeching. I have run over his tail, so I reverse to free it, followed by more screeching and now angry hissing. I have run over his tail again. I now lift my legs as I really think he is going to sink his teeth into them; he looked like he was going to. Between this and his screeching and hissing I drive the chair into the wall; the cat flees to the back door, and by the time I reach him he is licking his tail. He is okay. He has left behind his usual trademark, lots of fur. But give him time and he will get complacent again, and sitting comfortably on my power chair. Tuppence the Bold, or Tuppence the Bald. How clever is he really?

The natural enemy of the power chair

Life Nowadays

I now live in New Mexico, the red rock, the sunrises and the sunsets are stunning. I live here with my husband David, our cat Tuppence, Charlie our dog; and I can't forget we also have 5 sheep, 4 lambs and 5 chickens which David looks after. He also has to look after me too, so all the things that I can't do anymore, or let's say I try but to no avail — opening boxes, doing the laundry; anything that involves muscles or strength, David has to do for me. I bent down in my power chair in the kitchen to pick something up from the floor, and got stuck and had to shout for David's help.

All my family are still in Scotland, and my aunt is on the east coast of the USA, so I'm truly thankful for Skype, texting and Facebook. Skype really shortens the miles and Facebook keeps me up-to-date with family and friends on a daily basis.

Tuppence the cat now moves out of the way, he's probably had enough of getting his tail caught, and the pain, and he's only got so much more fur he can lose before he has bald patches. Now I look behind my chair and check he's not lying behind it on the floor. Now he slips past me at the side of my power chair; I thought cats were meant to be clever, not this one. Perhaps he has trouble "thinking outside of the box".

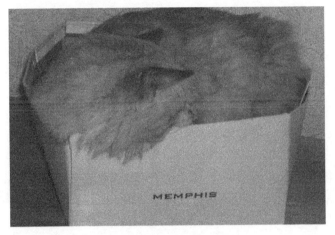

Tuppence thinking inside of the box

Life has changed and I have to adapt, do the best I can; it does take me longer to do things. If that isn't bad enough, I give myself more work trying to do something that I think I can do. That can be a small thing like aiming to put something in the bin and I miss the bin completely and it's just inches away. There are some things I can't do now at all i.e. walk unaided, carry bags, pull most weeds, open most packets of food. I find scissors, jar openers, self-pull can openers are all very helpful; and of course the first thing I thought, "This is great, grated cheese," and also the spell-checker on the computer!

I don't do as much as I used to, it seems to take ages to do the simplest things. To let Charlie out, feed Tuppence and make myself a cuppa, I noticed the other day took me 20 minutes. I can do more if I sit down and don't have to walk; it feels like my legs have been filled up with cement.

I probably over-think things. If I have to walk with my walker, just the thought of how long it will take and the effort it takes can put me off. Using my chair is okay until I think of getting out of it to do anything, which can put me off of doing things. Doing dishes or cooking etc. while sitting down is hopeless, and standing for more than a few seconds is too much, but I do stand as at least it exercises my legs and there is some who can't do that, and I'm not at that stage yet. I do have a stationary bike for exercise.

I seem to be robbed of doing the ironing too now. First walking unaided, now this. Now trying to iron a shirt and a pair of jeans has become a balancing act and dangerous. The iron wobbled too many times when I leaned on the ironing board for support. I remember ironing for a friend for 6 hours, I really was one of those people who ironed everything and loved ironing, but now another thing bites the dust.

There is a ramp at the front of the house which I use now (compliments of the Muscular Dystrophy Association) and I can still drive. The only reason I don't drive as much as some is because I don't really have a love of driving, and my husband likes driving so I don't argue about that one. The dents and smashed rear light probably have something to do with it too — that's not because of my ataxia; reversing is just not my strong point.

I managed to do some ironing yesterday, albeit it was from my power chair, sitting down to iron, never would have thought I would do that, and while I was ironing I actually felt like I was okay, my old self. I didn't have to think about what I was doing; not having to think about my balance, falling, having to try and move things about the ironing board and the iron wobbling, and me toppling and everything else with me; it really was so liberating. I might only be able to do a few items but hey I can iron! You'd think I had won a holiday or something, it was so great to be able to iron.

It's not easy accepting things you used to be able to do and you'd take for granted that you could do them. Accepting how things are now can be a tearful time, anyway for me it is. Recently even sitting for a period of time and doing nothing can tire me out. I have noticed over the last few weeks I watch more TV or am on the computer. Watching anything (talk about time-consuming) that doesn't involve having to get up is more appealing to me now.

Things can become overwhelming now; little things that I used to be able to do without getting upset are now so daunting, and too much to handle. A few months ago my husband was bed-ridden with 'flu and unable to eat. After a few days he fancied a pancake, and I used to make pancakes by the plate-load; the kids would eat them as soon as the pancakes hit the plate.

I planned to make just about four pancakes, easy stuff, so I trotted off to the kitchen with my walker, all raring to go. I got to the kitchen, which is only about 20 feet away, but now I was tired out with walking just that few feet. The dog needed to be fed too, and with pancakes to make, and our lovely cat lying on a kitchen chair sleeping is then sick, all over the chair and the kitchen floor, which as it is linoleum, the sick then proceeds to continue on underneath the table. I fell to my knees sobbing like a baby; it was way too much to handle. It was going to take me a lot longer and by now I was much too tired.

My husband and I eat out a lot more, and it is really the only time he eats well. I could just nibble on things but he can't, he needs to eat a full meal. I can't cook like I used to, because standing at the cooker is unsafe and if I do start, after a bit the thought of what I still have to do is too much. If I over-tire myself I don't want to eat either, I just want to cry or rest. That can be the stubborn part of me, "Yeah, I can do this," but then reality kicks in; too late I've already started then I'm stuck and halfway to finished, usually it takes even longer now.

I like to make a big batch of burritos (mine have bacon, egg, cheese and sausage in them, all cooked, and then it's rolled up in a tortilla). I wrap them individually in foil and then freeze them so when you want one, just take it out of the freezer and put it straight in the oven for about 20-25 minutes at about 300-350F. This is using a toaster oven. You might need to adjust it to your requirements.

When you make a meal and there's extra, put the extra on a paper plate, cover it and freeze it and have it for another time. You can put food in containers and freeze them. However putting the extra food on a paper plate can save you time in long run. You take the paper plate out of the freezer and you slide it onto a foil dish pan, cover the foil pan with foil and stick it in the oven. No dirty pans or plates to wash.

I have heard of bananas (for potassium), magnesium and tonic water to alleviate cramps. There are pharmaceutical medicines you can take for any symptoms you might have, but I haven't had to take any as yet but that could change in the future. I will cross that bridge if or when I come to it.

Last year a friend organized a day at a spa. It was a four hour drive to just get there. "Yes, I'll go." I was really looking forward to it. Then later that day I started to think, "How do I get from the changing rooms to the pools? How do I even get into the water safely?" were some questions I thought of. I had to cancel, I couldn't go. Later I found out it wouldn't have been safe for me, because they weren't handicapped accessible.

I try to go to bed earlier and get up later than I used to, another perk of having ataxia; rest and sleep definitely help. I have found after I get up in the morning I can stay up for about 6-7 hours then I have to go for a snooze or at least a lie down (level out). If I fall asleep it's normally for about 2 hours. There is a difference between being tired physically and being tired mentally.

After a snooze or lie down in the day, normally for me I am then mentally rested but can still get tired physically very easily. This happens to me round about 3-5pm. Sometimes I sit on a recliner so as not to fall asleep; I can get annoyed at myself if I sleep, what I can do in 2 hours, I don't want/need to sleep that long. Oh really, your body is telling you something different. If I don't take notice of the warning signals then most of the time you can meet the floor or walls. The more tired you are the more likely you are to feel wobbly. After a nap, then I am awake for another 6-7 hours, then it's usually bed time.

I try to get to bed no later than 10pm so David has time to himself; he is usually on the computer by then and so doesn't have to worry so much about what I am doing — falling, or tripping over the fresh air (now that's an art!)

He knows I am in bed so I should be safe. If I have been busy the previous day, the next day I stay asleep longer.

Some other things I have found really helpful are grab bars, they're on the wall beside the shower (it's a bathtub with shower). I really wonder how I or anyone managed without them. In fact we have banisters to put on the walls so that it will be safer for me when I go anywhere in the house that my power chair or walker can't go.

I do have a portable "save-er" grip bath and shower handle which works on sinks, tiles, most flat surfaces. You can take it with you anywhere; it has suction pads on each end of the handle and it is between 10-11 inches long; it's sturdy although it is not a grab bar to put all your weight on, but it is strong. It cost under $20, so well worth it.

I use a straw to drink cold drinks like water, juice or iced coffee, but not for hot drinks. I eat a lot of the time now using a spoon; I have cutlery that can be bent to your requirements and a knife that is more rounded to make cutting easier (I was told a pizza cutter is good for cutting however I haven't tried that yet).

I have a two-handled mug, a glasses case with two handles (like a mini handbag), which are easy for opening — you pull on the handles to open, easier on your hands and wrists if you have weakness there. I have noticed the muscles in the bottom part of my arms and at the wrists get achy after just a few minutes use now, and that can be something as basic as picking up a cup of tea.

Swivel cushions help on hard chairs, so you can turn about without having to move the whole chair. A gripper bar, this helps when you have to pick up or reach for something, and it's not for heavy stuff because you are holding whatever it is you are picking up or reaching for and the gripper bar.

A stylus pen I can use for touch screens and things that have small keyboards, like my cellphone, computer and printer. I have problems with typing, so I tend to hit more than one key now. I've got my own spelling, but at least I can read it. I know what I'm trying to say, it just doesn't seem to appear that way, so I don't text as much now, I'm quicker just phoning. My handwriting is now like a scribble and that is after only a few words, and then becomes unreadable even to me. Speaking of texting, and people texting while walking — they're coming right towards you; you're the one trapped in the power chair who can't get out of their way in a hurry. It is not safe for them or you if there is a collision, so usually you or someone else has to stop them. Honestly I think even a bucket of water thrown over them wouldn't halt them or wake them up; they seem oblivious to their surroundings.

I try to avoid slippery surfaces, like wet floors, wooden floors, ice, anything that moves too i.e. tablecloths, rugs, wet leaves, and lean-on paper on a desk or table, etc. — oh, and <u>crowds</u>!

One place I don't go in to is a public toilet; I go before I leave home, and hold it in until I get back home. The doors for the toilets are usually too heavy for me now, to keep open while I try and maneuver through them. The hand towels/drier or the bin are usually not beside the wash basins, and it's dangerous walking on drips of water left by other people on the floor on their way to dry their hands. Not to mention that most handicapped toilets are the farthest away. I imagine some toilets would be okay, but it seems very few would be, so why take a risk trying them. If you have someone to hold the door to the toilets open for you it does help a lot (thank you David). Portaloos, forget it — for me anyway. If you're bursting and able-bodied then needs must, having scent on a tissue helps. If you really have to.

I liked swimming too, my uncle taught me when I was about 5 years old. Now I won't go near water, unless it was a toddler pool so that if I fell in the water at least I'd get on my knees so my head would be above the water. I could use a swimming ring or arms bands, yeah so I will

I don't have to take any prescription medicine, only vitamin D3, CQ10, fish oil and B12. I would try natural remedies first to see if they helped; I don't want to have to take another medicine to counteract a medicine that I have already been prescribed.

I attend the monthly MDA group meetings and find them friendly and encouraging. Most days I go on the online group. Some of their comments are so funny, you can relate with most of them. It can be helpful too as the best place to get answers from is someone who knows what this is like as they have ataxia as well.

Another thing that seems to be happening now is the issue about lying down and then getting up. I can be okay when I am up on my feet, but give it a few minutes then I start to feel faint and clammy. If I don't get to a lying-down position immediately I think I would collapse wherever I am. I usually lie down with my little fan on and then after about ten minutes I'm okay. I just take things a little slower on arising if I remember to, as if I didn't go slow enough without this happening. This has happened before, since I was in my teens, only there were years in between, now it's a few months apart. Before I had even heard of it, I had read that this can also be a symptom of MSA. Oh and how could I forget that my hands and especially my feet and the bottom part of my legs now feel or get cold. Another move I do now is like a pigeon when it's walking and its head moves back and forth. That happens when anyone comes near my face, Doctor, nurse, eye Doc, hairdresser etc. Oh, the joys!

Hobbies

I can still knit and sew; only the other day I was off buying material, having to go around the material shop in a wheelchair. If I didn't go to the shop, I'd have to go on-line. Cheaper going to the shop.

I've knitted since I was 5 or 6 years old; my nana taught me. The sewing crafts, I learnt about two and a half years ago. The sewing I have to do a bit at a time; it can take me weeks or months to finish something. I usually need help with the cutting. It works out quicker getting someone to help me with the cutting.

I call my sewing and knitting projects "unique", nothing like them. I would never be able to make a living off them or show them. However when I was at our State Fair in September 2015, there was a display of craft work that had been made by disabled people. So hopefully I plan to do something for next year and show that. Just because we might have a disability doesn't mean we can't do a craft. I like to sew but next to the quilts on display, eh not a chance of making anything like theirs, they're flawless. I left the display of quilts, then I saw the display by disabled people and my spirit was lifted. So there is a place for my unique sewing.

I did this little piper about three years ago, I could then and still can knit, only it takes me longer now. It had its awkward bits to knit. I wouldn't be in a hurry to knit that again. I felt really emotional when I mailed him as I had got really attached to him.

It took me a few months to knit him at the pace I went. My aunt called him "Angus" — that is the name of the county we're from — so it's very appropriate for him to be given that name.

The table topper (known as the Dresden plate design). I made this in November 2015 for my mum to go on her coffee table at Christmas time (I hope it fits). It's different, can't be bought at a store, and has been made by her daughter.

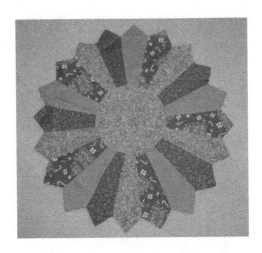

This is one of two baby quilts I made in August 2015. The only difference is the other quilt has yellow instead of the blue.

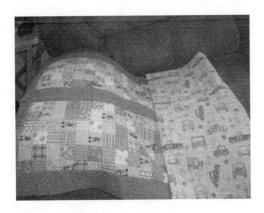

I can still knit and sew, I am thankful that I still can, not at the usual standard but recognizable to me, there one of a kind, unique.

My hope is in Jesus Christ; I couldn't get through this without Him. He is with me now to the end, and then I'm off to Him.

This verse gives me a lot of comfort:

"And lo, I am with you always, *even* to the end of the age." (*Matthew 28:20*)

Amen.

CPSIA information can be obtained
at www.ICGtesting.com
Printed in the USA
FSHW011357141219
65092FS